Meet Me in Malaga

Caitlin Maggs

Presentation by *BookLeaf Publishing*

Web: www.bookleafpub.com

E-mail: info@bookleafpub.com

ISBN: 9789358313871

First edition 2023

This is specially dedicated to my Grandpa,
Peter Costen. Thank you for your walks, your
talks and your love. You were the goodest man,
my inspiration to help the world and the
reminder that I, and everyone, are special.

Thank you endlessly.

ACKNOWLEDGEMENT

Thank you to my family, my whole world - my Mum, my Dad, my Grandparents and my three incredible sisters. You are everything to me.

PREFACE

Meet me in the Midnight Morn, where something new stirs between every sip and wave.

Meet Me in Malaga

Meet me in Malaga

where palms
lick the sun
with green tongues.

Lemon ice cream
drips

and all
is orange.

Orange curtains
remind you
and make you
forget

The sun is more than
A colour here

and the sea
blushes sunset pink

when you admire
too long

Women dance
Salsa smooth

Parrots
sing away
concrete thoughts

and now
in this Malaga sea
it's only me
and me
for company

and on our
final night,
we are greedy

for more
and more
colour

we stuff ourselves
silly

shell-searching
for fireworks
in the sea.

Is a Home Place or People?

3

Lime trees
look on
your leafy walk
as the lady lined
with time
crosses your
path

The stranger
casts a familiar smile

on your homesick
hunger

she feeds
and leaves you

rumbling
in her stroller
sits a poodle

you pick up her
umbrella

A pop

A pang
A wave

she is here
like a mirror memory

A dove
dips into sight
watching too
this evening's
exchange

she smiles.
You smile

and walk on

Have you been here
before?

How to Draw a Peace Dove

5

Kind eyes
are deep on a dove,
like an old friend
you've not met yet,
but always known

Putting pen
to paper
too soon

- now it's flown.

Like a sword
sharpened after battles
have taken

That's what you get

choosing war
over patience

Impossible to draw;
a Picasso Pigeon

La Taberna Del Obispo, Malaga

Strange words
hang familiar
like a hug

Birds bathe in beauty,
washing feathers in
medieval memory

and cats nap
in history's slippers.

You sigh away old ghosts
and sharpen your pencils
in this Spanish
coffee shop.

Midnight Morn

The sun sweats
in our hands
holding tight
today

Our tears
are souvenirs

still-sealed
in plastic bags

We had a thousand days today

All eyes
Are glued and glossy

Pavements
are rougher in London

Oaks guard tall
no space for palms
hanging back
breezy.

You haven't unpacked

In Piccadilly walking
with sand in my shoes

All is pain and magic
In this midnight morn.

Spanish Latte

9

Take a sip
and sit
with me

Spanish latte,
for two?

Where

10

Next?

Blackberry Picking

Black
and blue
and too full
of juices

you stuff handfuls
into pockets
and jars

Sweet
and sharp
they burst
and bleed
sweet

squeezing seasons
and seeds
into jams
preserved.

You lick
your fingers
for one more taste
of today.

Ground me to the moon;

12

I have found you.

Somerset Sun

Crunch of snow,
Like a piece of toast.
We walk. We chew
on our thoughts
Together and alone.
Me and my grandpa
Still have far to go

To fill our mouths
With words, weather
-talk in our winter worlds.

On this day of days
He lends me his coat.
Tartan tobacco, we smile.
You've changed. So have you

I hear him think,
Where has she gone?

Laughing away
In the Somerset sun.

We sigh in secret.
Snow drifting between us.
We trudge on.

Inches apart
Feels like miles
What can we do?
Time must have tricked us,
As we tire of remember-when's
And feeding ducks,
Of blackberry fields
And chasing sails.
When here and now
We slip into silence

Walking on
In the frosting sun.

Cover-Up

Passing through

in the queue
you stand -
'that's my wife's name!'
'Is that your name?
A couple spot my wounded
arm.

How strange;
I can hear them thinking.

'Do you have Arabic family?'
Curiosity.

Not enough to pry
but enough to wonder;
What does it mean?

And back to that day
a daily reminder
In the mirror
I am mad

I got tattooed
as she pulled a face.

Her name.
Like a bullet.
ink on my skin.
Passing through.

As if to say;
better you than me
- if only you know how
temporary you'd be.

The Girl That Got Away

Finding words
for woes is hard

Like searching for shells
in a sea of stones

Until that time
my words fly

flowing free
from my wrist ink
onto paper
rivers.

Pain pouring
into beauty and oceans
Of common magic
matter

In a paper meadow,
yes. We can dance
here.

And I can see myself
Again in my reflection.

Don't mind me

Sleeping beneath the sea

Emotions
and oceans
weigh me.

Until the mermaid
finds her feet.

Now I tumble
and trudge through
sodden sand

And I forget you
but remember who

Broke my words
before you
broke my shore

Long before
you tumbled through
too

And spoke.

Contactless

Tuesday
10am
Jubilee Line

Flinching
Blinking
too many people

Too many smells
and noises
to swallow

You move underground
to a man begging
for change
to eat

As Westminster
sleeps

Languages chatter
in accepted closed
tongues.
Purses clutched
noses hidden in scarves
and under T-shirts

As the man
stretching his toes
stretches his arms
down the carriage

Reaching
Pleading

Arms bruised
Dirt Lines like tyre marks
Up and down
Both arms

An apple's exchanged

Same script
New story

Eyes down
Purses clutched
Toes bent
Pressed hard to the
carriage rumble

Flinching
Blinking

Pay contactless

and mind the gap

Next station: Westminster

October

Autumn fell
like a curtain

No ice cream
at this interval
but black coffee

Steaming bus windows,
kids draw faces
with their fingers
and glasses
unclear

of which stop is next

All but the smile
on a baby

colours flapping
like hands
at curtain call
down from the tree

West Bank 2013

Tracing bullet holes
with my finger
along a wall

Stories I cannot hear
but I listen

Punctured
by politics

on doormats
and faces

Delirious
Decades

A crack
in the glass of
our watch

1948

You wish the world
would watch

Roofless
Hospitality
makes me cry

A mother passes
me a glass
of orange squash

as the snow
descends on
the desert.

Magic Me

I could colour the world
with thoughts of you

and the world would follow

As I follow
you

Your colours that colour
me

I love you,
I love you
like a scorch of a star
and a beat in the
heart.

Magic me into
Your heart

I am yours

A million times over

I am yours

I am yours
I am yours

Name:

27

Saved as Friend.

Wonderful Problem

28

Books are thoughts cemented

and paper cuts

Maida Vale W9

A woman shoves
past me
with places to see
and people to be

Maida Vale W9

Rich rise from
their beds

Ready for their
Coffee order.

Prepaid.

Dog walkers
pace, polished
and proper
as their poodle
in front

What is missing?

I found me

I chased my heart
up and down the country

and kept running after.

I chased my heart
up and down the country

And came back to me.